Published in 2014 by The Rosen Publishing Group, Inc.
29 East 21st Street, New York, NY 10010

First Edition

Editor: Jennifer Way
Book Design: Kate Vlachos
Photo Research: Katie Stryker

Photo Credits: Cover alfotokunst/Shutterstock.com; p. 4 Kues/Shutterstock.com; p. 5 M. Niebuhr/ Shutterstock.com; p. 6 Webspark/Shutterstock.com; p. 7 (left) iPics/Shutterstock.com; p. 7 (right) Chris K Horne/Shutterstock.com; p. 8 Alexey Kamenskiy/Shutterstock.com; p. 9 Darren J. Bradley/Shutterstock.com; pp. 10, 14 Siim Sepp/Shutterstock.com; p. 11 Andrea Danti/Shutterstock.com; p. 12 Thierry Hennet/Flickr/ Getty Images; p. 13 Kristal Leonard Photography/Flickr/Getty Images; p. 15 optimarc/Shutterstock.com; p. 16 Nickolay Stanev/Shutterstock.com; p. 17 (left) Stas Moroz/Shutterstock.com; p. 17 (right) Melinda Fawver/Shutterstock.com; p. 18 The Power of Forever Photography/E+/Getty Images; p. 19 Krzysztof Wiktor/Shutterstock.com; pp. 20–21 Imfoto/Shutterstock.com; p. 22 Claudio Rossol/Shutterstock.com.

Publisher's Cataloging Data

Dee, Willa.
Unearthing igneous rocks / Willa Dee. — 1st ed. — New York : Power Kids Press, c2014
        p. cm. — (Rocks: the hard facts)
Includes an index.
ISBN: 978-1-4777-2901-4 (Library Binding) — ISBN: 978-1-4777-2990-8 (Paperback) —
ISBN: 978-1-4777-3060-7 (6-pack)
1. Igneous rocks—Juvenile literature. 2. Petrology—Juvenile literature. 3. Magmatism—Juvenile literature. I. Title.
QE461 .D44 2014
552.'1
Manufactured in the United States of America

CPSIA Compliance Information: Batch #W14PK4: For Further Information contact Rosen Publishing, New York, New York at 1-800-237-9932

CONTENTS

ALL ABOUT IGNEOUS

On Earth's **surface**, rocks are everywhere. There are also rocks below Earth's surface! Igneous rocks are one of Earth's three kinds of rocks. The other two are sedimentary rocks and metamorphic rocks. Igneous rocks, sedimentary rocks, and metamorphic rocks all form in different ways. However, all of Earth's rocks are made up of **minerals**.

This picture shows granite, which is a type of igneous rock. Your kitchen counter might be made out of granite.

Basalt is a type of igneous rock that is used to make statues. It can be found at the bottom of the ocean and near volcanoes.

The word "igneous" comes from the Latin word for "fire," *ignis*. Igneous rocks form from cooled-down magma or lava. Magma is a hot **molten** material found below Earth's **crust**. Lava is magma that has pushed up through Earth's crust to its surface. You can find igneous rocks above and below Earth's surface.

EARTH'S LAYERS

Earth is not one solid piece of rock all the way through. It has **layers**. At the center of Earth is the core. The core has two parts. The inner core is at Earth's very center, and the outer core is around it. Scientists think the inner core is solid metal. The outer core is liquid metal. Earth's core is extremely hot.

CRUST
3–25 miles (5–40 km) thick

MANTLE
2,200 miles (3,540 km) thick

OUTER CORE
1,400 miles (2,253 km) thick

INNER CORE
800 miles (1,287 km) thick

This diagram shows Earth's layers. Under Earth's oceans, the crust is only 3 to 5 miles (5–8 km) thick. The part of the crust that makes up Earth's land is up to 25 miles (40 km) thick.

Above: You can see the spot on Earth's surface where the North American Plate and the Eurasian Plate, two of Earth's tectonic plates meet, in this picture. The North American and Eurasian Plates are the second- and third-largest plates. *Right*: This part of Earth's crust in Hawaii is made up of land and ocean waters.

The next layer is Earth's mantle. The mantle is cooler than Earth's core but still very hot. The mantle is a mix of solid rock and molten rock. Earth's hard outer layer is called the crust. Earth's crust is made of several **tectonic plates** of rock that fit together like a puzzle.

SOLID TO LIQUID TO SOLID

Rocks on Earth's surface seem very hard. However, if they are heated up enough, they can melt into a liquid! The high heat needed to melt rock is found only deep inside Earth.

The tectonic plates that make up Earth's crust move very slowly over time.

Lava is liquid rock on Earth's surface. The lava flowing from this volcano in Hawaii turns into solid igneous rock when it hits the water of the Pacific Ocean and cools.

The Vasquez Rocks, in California, were formed when two plates hit and rock from one was pushed up over the other. Rock from the bottom plate was pushed down and melted into magma.

As the plates move, rock from Earth's surface is pulled down below the crust. The rock gets hotter and hotter as it moves deeper and deeper. When the rock reaches between 1,100 and 2,400° F (593–1,316° C), it melts into magma.

Magma, or molten rock, does not stay liquid forever. If magma cools down enough, it turns into igneous rock.

LAVA AND VOLCANOES

Magma is melted rock trapped below Earth's surface. However, magma can push up through cracks in Earth's crust. When it reaches the surface, it flows out as lava.

Often, magma does not break through to the surface right away. It collects in a magma **chamber**. Over time, more magma collects.

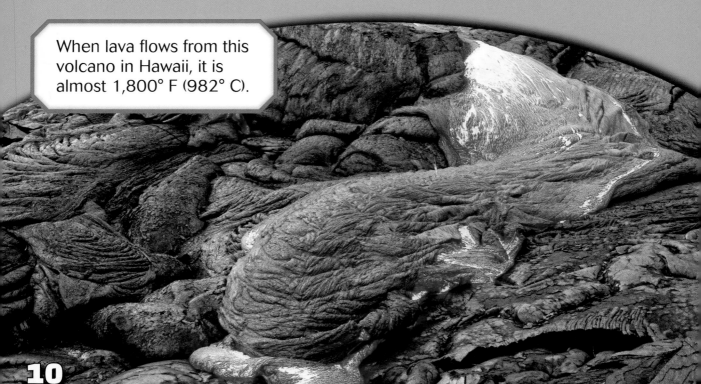

When lava flows from this volcano in Hawaii, it is almost 1,800° F (982° C).

This is a diagram of a volcanic eruption. You can see lava, ash, and gases coming out of the volcano.

GASES

LAVA

ASH

LAYERS OF IGNEOUS ROCK AND ASH

MAGMA CHAMBER

EARTH'S CRUST

Pressure builds inside the chamber. When there is enough pressure, magma, gases, and **ash** quickly push up through to the surface. This is called a volcanic eruption.

When lava cools down on Earth's surface, it forms volcanic igneous rock. Over time, lava flows and ash from eruptions can also form different kinds of volcanoes. These include shield volcanoes and cinder cones.

EXTRUSIVE ROCKS

Igneous rock that forms from lava has two different names. It is called volcanic rock because lava flows from volcanoes. It can also be called extrusive rock. This means it is igneous rock that has formed on the surface of Earth's crust.

This picture shows Landmannalaugar, a mountain range in southern Iceland. The range is very colorful. Its colors include pink, brown, green, yellow, blue, purple, black, and white!

The rock cliffs in this picture are made of rhyolite. They are in the Grand Canyon of Yellowstone, in Wyoming.

Lava cools into igneous rock quickly. The minerals in the lava do not have time to grow into larger **crystals** before cooling. This makes extrusive igneous rock fine grained.

The most common kind of extrusive rock is basalt. Basalt is glassy and black or gray in color. Another kind of extrusive rock is rhyolite. Rhyolite is light in color, ranging from white to pink.

Not all magma reaches Earth's surface as lava. Magma that stays trapped inside Earth's crust can also become igneous rock. This kind of igneous rock is called intrusive rock. It can take a very long time for intrusive igneous rock to form.

This picture shows diorite inside granite. When a smaller rock is inside a larger rock, it is called a xenolith.

Granite is a material that is often used in construction. Tile floors, desktops, and gravestones can be made out of granite.

It may take trapped magma thousands or millions of years to cool down enough to form rock.

When magma cools slowly, it gives minerals in the magma time to grow into crystals. This makes intrusive rock coarse grained. This means you can see crystals in the rock easily. Granite is one common kind of intrusive rock. Another is diorite.

MAKING MOUNTAINS

Earth's moving plates form many of Earth's mountains. Other mountains are formed from igneous rock.

Dome mountains form when magma pushes up against Earth's crust. However, this magma never reaches Earth's surface. It cools into a mound of intrusive rock below layers of surface rock. A dome on Earth's surface forms above the intrusive mound underneath.

Half Dome is a dome mountain in California. The mountain is called Half Dome because part of the dome fell away during an earthquake.

Left: You can see Half Dome in the back of this picture of Yosemite Valley. Yosemite Valley was carved out by the Merced River. *Below*: Millions of years ago, the granite rocks of the Sierra Nevada were buried deep underground. Erosion exposed them, making them a part of Earth's crust.

Other mountains are actually pieces of large intrusive rocks called plutons. Plutons reach Earth's surface when the rock above it is worn away through **erosion**. A gigantic pluton is generally made up of quartz or granite. Most of the Sierra Nevada, a mountain range in California and Nevada, was formed from one large pluton.

IN-BETWEEN ROCKS

Sometimes, magma almost reaches Earth's surface but does not flow out as lava. This rock is called subvolcanic igneous rock. Subvolcanic rock forms when magma cools just under Earth's surface. It does not form deep enough to be called intrusive rock. However, it does not form on Earth's surface, as extrusive rock does.

Devils Tower is a laccolith in Wyoming. It is 1,267 feet (386 m) tall! Only 4,000 of the mountain's 400,000 yearly visitors climb to the top.

Devils Tower is made out of igneous rock, but it is surrounded by different types of sedimentary rock, including sandstone, limestone, and shale.

Subvolcanic rocks are much less common than extrusive or intrusive igneous rocks.

One type of subvolcanic rock is called a laccolith. Laccoliths form in mushroom shapes between layers of sedimentary rock. Scientists think some parts of the Henry Mountains in Utah may be laccoliths.

MINERALS IN ROCK

Scientists also **classify** igneous rocks by the kinds of minerals in the rock. This means they look at the minerals in igneous rocks to put them into different groups.

Felsic rocks have a large amount of a mineral called silica. Lots of silica makes felsic rocks light in color. Granite is an example of an intrusive felsic rock. Rhyolite is an extrusive felsic rock.

Many things, like these beads, can be made out of igneous rocks. The green in these beads comes from ultramafic rock, which gets its color from the mineral olivine.

Mafic rocks have low amounts of silica. They also have high amounts of iron and magnesium. This combination of minerals makes mafic rock dark in color. Basalt is an extrusive mafic rock. Gabbro is an intrusive mafic rock.

PART OF THE CYCLE

Igneous rocks can be seen on Earth's surface and found under Earth's oceans. They are also trapped deep below Earth's crust. Wherever igneous rocks are, they will not stay igneous rocks forever. Igneous rocks are part of Earth's rock cycle, as are all rocks. Through this cycle, old rocks are broken down and new rocks form.

Over many years, igneous rocks can change into metamorphic rocks or sedimentary rocks. Over millions of years, erosion, heat, pressure, and melting change rocks from one kind to another. Earth's rock cycle never stops!

This lava is flowing into the ocean. When the lava cools, it will turn into igneous rock at the bottom of the ocean. The water level will rise. Rocks change our world!

GLOSSARY

ash (ASH) Pieces of tiny rock that shoot out of a volcano when it blows.

chamber (CHAYM-bur) A partly enclosed space like a room.

classify (KLA-seh-fy) To arrange in groups.

crust (KRUST) The outer, or top, layer of a planet.

crystals (KRIS-tulz) Patterns of many flat surfaces inside minerals.

erosion (ih-ROH-zhun) The wearing away of land over time.

layers (LAY-erz) Thicknesses of things.

minerals (MIN-rulz) Natural matter that is not animals, plants, or other living things.

molten (MOHL-ten) Made liquid by heat.

pressure (PREH-shur) A force that pushes on something.

surface (SER-fes) The outside of anything.

tectonic plates (tek-TO-nik PLAYTS) The different parts of Earth's crust that move very slowly over time.

INDEX

WEBSITES

Due to the changing nature of Internet links, PowerKids Press has developed an online list of websites related to the subject of this book. This site is updated regularly. Please use this link to access the list:

www.powerkidslinks.com/rthf/igneo/